Book Synopsis

"KINGDOM WATCHMAN - BUILDER OF THE WALL" provides advanced revelation and impartation on how to be an effective prayer ministry and prayer warrior, such that God's miracles, healings, and wonders consistently manifests in your life and the lives, ministries, and regions you pray for. Learn to position yourself to produce consistent answers from heaven, while ministering effectively in the areas of intercession, warfare, altar ministry, evangelism, salvation, deliverance, and the baptism of the Holy Spirit.

KINGDOM WATCHMAN WARFARE MANUAL I

TaquettaBaker@Kingdomshifters.com

(Website) Kingdomshifters.com

Connect with Taquetta via Facebook or YouTube

Copyright 2014 – Kingdom Shifters Ministries

All rights reserved. This book is protected by the copyright laws of the United States of America. This book may not be reprinted for commercial gain or profit. The use of occasional page copying for personal or group study is permitted and encouraged. Permission will be granted upon request.

Taquetta's Bio

Taquetta Baker is the founder of Kingdom Shifters Ministries (KSM). She has authored fourteen books and two decree CD's. Taquetta has a Master's Degree in Community Counseling with an emphasis on Marriage, Children and Family Counseling, a Bachelor's Degree in Psychology and Associates Degree in Business Administration. In addition, Taquetta has a Therapon Belief Therapist Certification from Therapon Institute and has 22 years of professional and Christian Counseling experience.

Taquetta is also gifted at empowering and assisting people with launching ministries, businesses and books and provides mentoring, counseling and vision casting through Kingdom Shifters Kingdom Wellness Program.
Taquetta serves on the Board of Directors for New Day Community Ministries, Inc. of Muncie, IN. In October 2008, Taquetta graduated from the Eagles Dance Institute under Dr. Pamela Hardy and received her license in the area of liturgical dance. Before launching into her own ministry, Taquetta served at her previous church for 12 years. She was a prophet, pioneer and leader of Shekinah Expressions Dance Ministry, teacher, member of the presbytery board, and overseer of the Altar Workers Ministry. Taquetta receives mentoring and ministry covering from Bishop Jackie Green, Founder of JGM-National PrayerLife Institute (Phoenix, AZ), and was ordained as an Apostle on June 7, 2014.

Taquetta flows through the wells of warfare and worship and mantles an apostolic mandate of judging and establishing God's kingdom in people, ministries, communities, and regions. Taquetta travels in foreign missions and throughout the United States. She has *mentored and established dance, altar workers, deliverance, and prophetic ministries. Taquetta ministers in the areas of fine arts, all manners of prayer, fivefold ministry, deliverance, healing, miracles, atmospheric worship, and empowers and train people in their destiny and life's vision.*

Connect with Taquetta and KSM at <u>kingdomshifters.com</u> or via Facebook. For more information regarding Bishop Jackie Green at Jgmenternational.org

Foreword

This book provides great revelation and impartation that will truly advance God's kingdom and shift people in being mature and knowledgeable regarding walking and operating His Spirit and calling upon their lives. The information regarding praying for others, working as a prayer team, being a builder of the wall, evangelizing, ministering salvation and the baptism of the Holy Spirit, and conducting deliverance ministry is practical, applicable, and will immediately increase the lives of any person or ministry who partakes of this revelation.

Every chapter holds powerful strategies and prayer tactics necessary to being an effective prayer warrior, to grow as an intercessor and in being able to consistently manifest God's miracles, healings, deliverance, signs, and wonders, while contending and establishing God's kingdom.

It has been my privilege to read this manual and to gleam from the fruit it entails. I am excited about activating what I have learned and look forward to imparting it into the lives of others.

Blessings,
Nina Cook
Taquetta's Spiritual Daughter

Table Of Contents

Nature & Character Of A Prayer Warrior 2
Prayer Ministry Qualifications.................................... 3
Skills & Training..5
Ministering With Power..6
Living Through A Spirit Of Readiness...........................9
Team Ministry..13
Unity Within The Prayer Ministry..............................15
Prayer Etiquette...27
Seeking God During Prayer Ministry............................29
Blessings Prayers During Times Of Uncertainty.................30
Ministering Salvation..31
Questions About Salvation.....................................32
Keys Regarding Salvation......................................32
Ministering To Someone Who Desires To Speak In Tongues.. 34
Hindrance To Speaking In Tongues..............................39
Leading Someone In Praying In Tongues.........................42
Purpose Of Deliverance Ministry...............................44
Demonic Manifestations..53
How To Cast Out Demons..56
Other Methods of Deliverance.................................. 57
Reasons Demons Stay...59

Nature & Character Of A Prayer Warrior

Dedicated

Reliable

Integral

Empathetic

Compassionate

Objective

Balanced

Loving & kind

Forgiving

Pursuer of deliverance and healing

Holy Spirit lead

Mindset of Christ

Obedient

Discerning

Disciplined

A leader

Administrative

A team player

Empowering of others

High moral character

Teachable

Constant learner

Operate in the Gift of Faith

Risk taker

Supernatural

Prayer Ministry Qualifications

- Operate in proven spiritual maturity
- Be known for psychological/emotional stability
- Have demonstrated love for and interest in people with a genuine expression of compassion at all times
- Operate in appropriate spiritual gifts such as Healing, Discernment, Helps, Exhortation or Encouragement, knowledge, wisdom, mercy; Spirit of Counsel, Understanding, Wisdom; Pastoral Care, Evangelism; Also Expressive knowledge of one's spiritual gifting/s (this can be taught in training)
- Possess adequate life experience
- Consistently attend meetings, trainings, prayer gatherings, prayer calls
- Be teachable
- Be committed to keeping and maintaining confidentiality (with exceptions to confidentiality usually including child abuse or elder abuse and danger to self or others).
    - A. Confidentiality is essential in prayer ministry. The only time you can break confidentiality is if a person is a threat to themselves or others, and even then you must direct the matter to leadership and they will follow through with how to handle the matter.
    - B. Do not take it upon yourself to report issues to families, the police or legal services. These matters must go through your pastors first and they will give further direction if necessary on how to handle it.
- Have no past/present history of child or elder abuse allegations or charges or rape charges or allegations

- Be rooted in the Word and have a lifestyle aligned to the Word of God
- Be submitted to leadership and in tune with the church's vision and yearly missions statement
- Be open to investing in development through literature, conferences, etc.

Skills & Training

Prayer Warriors should be able to minister in the following areas:

- Ministering Salvation
- Ministering the Baptism of the Holy Spirit (Speaking In Tongues)
- Baptismal Ministry (Ministering to someone who desires to be baptized)
- A level of Deliverance Ministry & Spiritual Warfare
- Discerning when to use or acquire assistance in various spiritual giftings such as healing, discernment, helps, etc.
- Discerning the necessity for Counseling & Deliverance Referrals
- Being able to effectively move about the altar, work the altar, praise and worship, and access leadership and other altar workers when necessary
- Understanding the Apostolic & Prophetic vision of the church
- Understanding the Vision of the prayer ministry

Ministering With Power

To minister with power, one should equip themselves with the following tools:
- Be filled with the Holy Spirit
- Study and memorize scripture and bible stories so you can use them to empower people and as a weapon against the enemy
- Live a life of fasting and prayer
- Use the name of Jesus
- Use the blood of Jesus
- Use the fire of the Holy Spirit
- Use the glory of God
- Learn and ask God for other spiritual weapons
- Love and compassion is the greatest weapon. Ask God to give you His heart and to teach you and how to unconditionally love and walk in Godly compassion
- Consistently anoint yourself with oil
- Seek daily repentance and deliverance so you can be a pure well for God to flow through
- Learn and know the voice, heart, and feelings of God.
    A. Spend time in silence and in intimacy with God so you can learn and know His voice
    B. Learn when He is speaking through your five senses
    C. Learn when God is speaking through your body and body aches (this is the gift of knowledge at work)
    D. Learn when God is speaking through visions, dreams, and spiritual pictures
    E. Learn when God is speaking through the unwavering knowing He puts in you. This

is when you just confidently know God is saying, doing, feeling or wanting something even though He has not said a word. You simply know what He is speaking by His Spirit.
- F. Learn how to discern God through the atmosphere, climate, region and world around you.
- Consistently spend time with the Holy Spirit (God's presence), and soak yourself in the power of the Holy Spirit so His presence can be tangible in your life
- Seek God for all the gifts of the Holy Spirit that Paul listed in *1Corinthians 12*. These gifts are available to you as you "earnestly desire them" (*1Corinthians 12:31; 14:1*).
  - *A. Word of Wisdom* - God's supernatural perspective on how to achieve His will. God's knowledge rightly applied to specific situations.
  - *B. Word of Knowledge* - "Facts" given by God that are unknowable without revelation.
  - *C. The Gift of Faith* - The supernatural ability to believe God without doubt. Essential to the Gift of Healing and Miracles.
  - *D. The Gift of Healing* - Supernatural healing through special anointing of the Holy Spirit.
  - *E. The Working of Miracles* - A supernatural display of power that goes beyond the natural to counteract earthly and evil forces.
  - *F. Discerning of Spirits* - Spiritual insight into differences between the Holy Spirit, the spirit of Man, and evil spirits at work in the

earth; it is not the discerning of character faults or flaws.

G. *The Gift of Prophecy* - The forth-telling of God's utterance. It is not of the intellect but of the Spirit. It is divinely inspired and anointed words spoken by a believer.

H. *Divers Kinds of Tongues* - This is not to be confused with the use of tongues in private prayer or worship. This refers to the ministry of tongues to others. An utterance from a believer to another in a language unknown to the speaker. ***(Isaiah 28:11; Mark 16:17; Acts 2:4; 10:44-48; 19:1-7; 1Corinthians 12:10; 13:1-3; 14:2, 4-22, 26-31; 28:31)***

I. *Interpretation of Tongues* - Supernatural power to reveal the meaning of tongues. Not a translation, but an interpretation. Tongues and Interpretation working together can be the equivalent of prophecy.

- Learn about deliverance ministry and live a life of busting devils
- Always look to pray and encourage someone. The more you are open to be used, the easier it is to manifest miracles, signs, and wonders

Living Through A Spirit Of Readiness

- Prayer Warriors should come to church with a mindset and drive to produce miracles, signs and wonders for God's glory.
- I always say a bad church service is one where no one gets delivered, healed, saved, or set free. Prayer Warriors should enter church on the prowl to pray for someone.
- When it is your Sunday to be on duty, ask God throughout the week for words of knowledge, wisdom, counsel, understanding, prophecy, prayer strategies, specific assignments, etc., so you can strategically impact people's lives.
- Prayer Warriors should be on duty at least 30 minutes before service starts and remain on duty 30 minutes after service.

> **Romans 12:11** - *Never lag in zeal and in earnest endeavor; be aglow and burning with the Spirit, serving the Lord.*

- Remain upfront around the altar where people can distinguish that you are available for ministry. As this becomes the church's culture, you will find that many will seek prayer when coming to church overwhelmed and after contemplating what God dwelt with them on during the service. People will begin to pursue you because they will see your heart for ministry and desire to change lives for God's glory as His miracles, signs, and wonders follow you.
- This also opens the door for more miracles, healing and deliverance to take place. In addition, this can serve as a gateway for testimonies to

manifests that set the tone for services or spark revival after service is over.

2Timothy 4:2 - *Preach the word; be instant in season, out of season; reprove, rebuke, exhort with all longsuffering and doctrine.*

The Message Version - *So proclaim the Message with intensity; keep on your watch. Challenge, warn, and urge your people. Don't ever quit. Just keep it simple.*

Preaching means to proclaim the word. As Prayer Warriors, you are using your life and the portal of God's altar via prayer and encouragement to personally proclaim the word of God into peoples' lives and situations. Live a life through a constant readiness and pursuit to save, deliver, heal, and transform someone's life.

- While waiting for people to come for prayer, pray over the atmosphere.
    - A. Declare an open heaven over the people, church & region
    - B. Command a spirit of salvation, deliverance, healings, miracles, and transformation to invade the atmosphere
    - C. Release a quickening for people to be convicted, repenting, free before God, and hungry and submitted to change and glorifying Him.
    - D. Seek people to pray for and approach them as the Holy Spirit leads. As you pray this will cause the atmosphere to SHIFT into

subjection of seeking God, as people are less likely to lag or stand around and talk, if ministry is occurring. It will provoke them to prayer, worship, and even cause them to search if they need prayer. As this is cultivated in the church's culture, people will enter the sanctuary with a heart to be with God.

E. If church is over, hang out at the altar while searching God for people to minister to. Command all that went forth during the service to penetrate the kingdom of heaven and the hearts and atmosphere of the people. As you linger, this will draw some who desired ministry during church, yet did not embrace God's initial drawing. You can also approach people and ask them if you can minister to them. I did this all the time and God would do such miraculous works until it would spark what I call "church after church." As the people were getting breakthrough, those lingering in the church would begin to worship God for His workings, and it would cause others to go into prayer, praise and worship, and even pursue ministry for themselves. We have had countless people get baptized, filled with speaking in tongues, deliverance, miracles, and healings because of this strategy. I would always have altar lines after church because I had so activated these keys and had cultivated pursuing ways for God to use me for His glory, until people would seek me out for ministry. Jesus sought to minister and to do miracles for

God's glory. He has promised us that we would do greater than Him if we believe.

***John 14-12** - Verily, verily, I say unto you, He that believeth on me, the works that I do shall he do also; and greater works than these shall he do; because I go unto my Father.*

Team Ministry - Two By Two

- If at all possible, minister two by two. There is power in agreement. Jesus sent the disciples out two by two.

    Mark 6:7 - And he called unto him the twelve, and began to send them forth by two and two; and gave them power over unclean spirits

    Matthew 18:19 - Again I say unto you, That if two of you shall agree on earth as touching any thing that they shall ask, it shall be done for them of my Father which is in heaven.

- Working in sets of two allows for accountability should a person have a challenge with something that is said or done during ministry. If someone approach you for prayer, if possible, pull another prayer warrior or mature saint over to assist you. This may not always be possible but utilize it as much as you can. This is important in this age where people are quick to bring law suits and reproach upon ministries.
- Pairing also allows for a greater measure of the presence of the Lord to operate as the two can work as a team, search God together and offer more effective ministry.
- At my previous assembly I would use this tool to train new prayer warriors who wanted to be used to pray and encourage others. I would pair them with a mature prayer warrior and then they would receive hands on training on how to operate in their giftings and effectively minister to others. The more people you can train to effectively minister to

others, the greater God can be glorified. This also equips people to minister and diminishes issues where people become offended due to receiving false prophecies, words of error, inappropriate or non-effective ministry, etc.

Unity Within The Prayer Ministry

Unity among a prayer ministry is essential for the effectiveness of the ministry.

> *Psalms 133 - Behold, how good and how pleasant it is for brethren to dwell together in unity! It is like the precious oil upon the head, running down on the beard, the beard of Aaron, Running down on the edge of his garments. It is like the dew of Hermon, Descending upon the mountains of Zion; for there the Lord commanded the blessing – Life forevermore.*

The scripture encourages us to come to attention by beholding how good and how pleasant it is for brethren to dwell together in unity. The word:

- **B. Good** denotes that there is wealth and potential present
- **C. Pleasant** denotes an enjoyment, a delight, an agreement and even that an agreeing atmospheric sound is present (Where there is chaos and division, the agreement and atmospheric sound is erratic).
- **D. Brethren** denotes that we are all in relationship with one another and that we resemble one another in some fashion or likeness.

Dictionary.com defines "unity" as:
1. the state of being one; oneness
2. a whole or totality as combining all its parts into one
3. the state or fact of being united or combined into one, as of the parts of a whole; unification

4. absence of diversity; unvaried or uniform character.
5. oneness of mind, feeling, etc., as among a number of persons
6. concord, harmony, or agreement

The Psalms not only tells us to unify, but to dwell together in unity.

The word *dwell* denotes a continual occurrence that has no ending.

The Hebrew word for *dwell* is "*yasab*" and means "*to inhabit, abide, remain, to sit, to stay, and also to marry.*"

Though we know the importance of unity as it relates to gathering together, having like hearts, mindsets, visions, giftings, etc., we never really consider the concept of unity being one of a great bond where we stay among one another and in tune with one another to a degree of marriage - of covenant. This definitely yields revelation of the reason worldly gangs and cults have blood in-blood out covenants. The agreement is essentially equated to giving yourself to marriage - and marriage is for life - the unity has no earthly end. Generally one marries in life and until death.

Spiritually the concept of being married to a group does not mean remaining bonded to that group forever. However, as God places a person in that ministry, one should be dedicated to God's purpose and be a blessing to the ministry. I guess we could contend that there should be a mindset of spiritual connectedness in relations to exuding the love, unity and respect portrayed in a marriage. God should be the head, the leader should be submitted, hear and obey God, and the people should follow the leader as he or she hears and follows God.

We are all required to pray as it builds our relationship with God and provides an avenue for Him to establish His kingdom in the earth. In this light, God may use a person in intercession and warfare, but that does not mean they are to be a part of a prayer ministry. Someone who is called to a prayer ministry sacrifices His or her personal pet peeves, dislikes of others, critical spirit, personal judgments, and pride, for the good of the ministry.

> ***Romans 15:1-7*** - *We then that are strong ought to bear the infirmities of the weak, and not to please ourselves. Let every one of us please his neighbour for his good to edification. For even Christ pleased not himself; but, as it is written, the reproaches of them that reproached thee fell on me. For whatsoever things were written aforetime were written for our learning, that we through patience and comfort of the scriptures might have hope.*
>
> *Now the God of patience and consolation grant you to be likeminded one toward another according to Christ Jesus: That ye may with one mind and one mouth glorify God, even the Father of our Lord Jesus Christ. Wherefore receive ye one another, as Christ also received us to the glory of God.*
>
> ***The Amplified Version*** - *WE WHO are strong [in our convictions and of robust faith] ought to*

> *bear with the failings and the frailties and the tender scruples of the weak; [we ought to help carry the doubts and qualms of others] and not to please ourselves. Let each one of us make it a practice to please (make happy) his neighbor for his good and for his true welfare, to edify him [to strengthen him and build him up spiritually]. For Christ did not please Himself [gave no thought to His own interests]; but, as it is written, the reproaches and abuses of those who reproached and abused you fell on Me.*
>
> *Now may the God Who gives the power of patient endurance (steadfastness) and Who supplies encouragement, grant you to live in such mutual harmony and such full sympathy with one another, in accord with Christ Jesus, That together you may [unanimously] with united hearts and one voice, praise and glorify the God and Father of our Lord Jesus Christ (the Messiah). Welcome and receive [to your hearts] one another, then, even as Christ has welcomed and received you, for the glory of God.*

As a prayer ministry you serve as the foundation and the frontline army for the people, church and region **(Read Nehemiah 3).**

> ***Isaiah 62:6-7 The Amplified Version -*** *I have set watchmen upon your walls, O Jerusalem, who will never hold their peace day or night; you who [are His servants and by your prayers] put the Lord in remembrance [of His promises], keep not silence, And give Him no rest until He establishes Jerusalem and makes her a praise in the earth.*

Set is *Paqad* in the Hebrew and means, "*to be appointed officer, governor, judge, oversee, to avenge, charge, to be deposited.*"

Watchmen is *Samar* in the Hebrew and means, "*to guard, protect, keeper, give heed.*"

> **The Message Version** - *I've posted watchmen on your walls, Jerusalem. Day and night they keep at it, praying, calling out, reminding God to remember. They are to give him no peace until he does what he said, until he makes Jerusalem famous as the City of Praise.*

Dictionary.com defines "*wall*" as:

1. any of various permanent upright constructions having a length much greater than the thickness and presenting a continuous surface except where pierced by doors, windows, etc.: used for shelter, protection, or privacy, or to subdivide interior space, to support floors, roofs, or the like, to retain earth, to fence in an area, etc.
2. usually, walls, a rampart raised for defensive purposes
3. an immaterial or intangible barrier, obstruction, etc.
4. a wall-like, enclosing part, thing, mass, etc.: a wall of fire; a wall of troops
5. an embankment to prevent flooding, as a levee or sea wall
6. the outermost film or layer of structural material protecting, surrounding, and defining the physical limits of an object: the wall of a blood cell

As a prayer ministry you serve as a wall of protection - the barrier and fortitude - between the enemy and the people, church and region. Because of this position, you are the first ministry within the church/organization to encounter the enemy. If there are open doors in the prayer ministry due to disunity, it allows the enemy to attack what God has assigned you to protect. Though your personal life should definitely be in alignment with the Lord, unity within the ministry serves as the greatest weapon against Satan's attacks.

The reason Jesus had to come was because there was no one to properly work with God in intercession, truth, and justice, so that the wiles of the enemy could be dismantled and vanished.

> **Isaiah 59:16 -** *And He saw that there was no man and wondered that there was no intercessor [no one to intervene on behalf of truth and right]; therefore His own arm brought Him victory, and His own righteousness [having the Spirit without measure] sustained Him.*

God decided that He had to come in the form of man to complete this work.

> **Verse 17-19 -** *For he put on righteousness as a breastplate, and a helmet of salvation upon his head; and he put on the garments of vengeance for clothing, and was clad with zeal as a cloke. According to their deeds, accordingly he will repay, fury to his adversaries, recompence to his enemies; to the islands he will repay recompence. So shall they fear the name of the Lord from the*

west, and his glory from the rising of the sun. When the enemy shall come in like a flood, the Spirit of the Lord shall lift up a standard against him.

Jesus death and resurrection equipped us to be the standard - wall -against the enemy.

> ***Romans 6:5*** *- For if we have been planted together in the likeness of his death, we shall be also in the likeness of his resurrection.*
>
> ***Ephesians 6-10-18*** *- Finally, my brethren, be strong in the Lord, and in the power of his might. Put on the whole armour of God, that ye may be able to stand against the wiles of the devil. For we wrestle not against flesh and blood, but against principalities, against powers, against the rulers of the darkness of this world, against spiritual wickedness in high places. Wherefore take unto you the whole armour of God, that ye may be able to withstand in the evil day, and having done all, to stand.*
>
> *Stand therefore, having your loins girt about with truth, and having on the breastplate of righteousness; And your feet shod with the preparation of the gospel of peace; Above all, taking the shield of faith, wherewith ye shall be able to quench all the fiery darts of the wicked. And take the helmet of salvation, and the sword of the Spirit, which is the word of God: Praying always with all prayer and supplication in the Spirit, and watching thereunto with all perseverance and supplication for all saints;*

Ephesians 6:10-18, is speaking to a unified group of people as it begins by saying, "*Finally, my brethren.*" As we read on, we find that we are being dressed for war and our apparel and weaponry resemble the likeness to which God dressed Himself as Jesus in *Isaiah 59:17-19,* when He came to be the standard - wall against the enemy.

Jesus came to earth and stood in the natural realm against the enemy. Since Jesus is now seated on the right hand of God, and we are joint heirs to Him, we stand in the spirit realm against the enemy **(*Ephesians 2:6, Romans 8:17*)**.

We are the wall and if any area of the wall is damaged, offended, rotting, or crumbling due to division or discord, it allows opportunity for the enemy to gain a foothold in the people, church, and region.

Unity provokes the power of the Holy Spirit and releases God's promises and blessings:

> *Act 2:1-2 - And when the day of Pentecost was fully come, they were all with one accord in one place. And suddenly there came a sound from heaven as of a rushing mighty wind, and it filled all the house where they were sitting. And there appeared unto them cloven tongues like as of fire, and it sat upon each of them. And they were all filled with the Holy Ghost, and began to speak with other tongues, as the Spirit gave them utterance.*

Unity releases blessings and joy into the homes of those praying, the ministry, and in the region:

> ***Acts 2:46*** *- And they, continuing daily with one accord in the temple, and breaking bread from house to house, did eat their meat with gladness and singleness of heart.*
>
> ***Acts 4:24*** *- So when they heard that, they raised their voice to God with one accord and said: "Lord, You are God, who made heaven and earth and the sea, and all that is in them.*
>
> ***Acts 1:14*** *- These all continued with one accord in prayer and supplication, with the women and Mary the mother of Jesus, and with His brothers.*

Unity provokes consistent miracles signs and wonders to manifest:

> ***Acts 5:12*** *- And through the hands of the apostles many signs and wonders were done among the people. And they were all with one accord in Solomon's Porch.*
>
> ***Acts 8:6*** *- And the multitudes with one accord heeded the things spoken by Philip, hearing and seeing the miracles which he did.*

Unity breaks and transcends religious, traditional, racial, cultural, and political barriers, allowing the laws and will of inclusion, honor, and love to become the standard:

> ***2Corinthians 13:11-14*** *- Finally, brethren, farewell. Become complete. Be of good comfort, be*

> *of one mind, live in peace; and the God of love and peace will be with you. Greet one another with a holy kiss. All the saints greet you. The grace of the Lord Jesus Christ, and the love of God, and the communion of the Holy Spirit be with you all. Amen.*
>
> ***Galatians 3:26-28*** *- For you are all sons of God through faith in Christ Jesus. For as many of you as were baptized into Christ have put on Christ. There is neither Jew nor Greek, there is neither slave nor free, there is neither male nor female; for you are all one in Christ Jesus.*

Unity allows us to respect and esteem one another's giftings and callings and enables us to be equipped in a great fashion for the advancement and establishment of the kingdom of God:

> ***Ephesians 4:3-6*** *- Endeavoring to keep the unity of the Spirit in the bond of peace. There is one body and one Spirit, just as you were called in one hope of your calling; one Lord, one faith, one baptism; one God and Father of all, who is above all, and through all, and in you all.*
>
> ***Ephesians 4:11-16*** *- And He Himself gave some to be apostles, some prophets, some evangelists, and some pastors and teachers, for the equipping of the saints for the work of ministry, for the edifying of the body of Christ, till we all come to the unity of the faith and of the knowledge of the Son of God, to a perfect man, to the measure of the stature of the fullness of Christ; that we should no longer be children, tossed to and fro and carried*

> *about with every wind of doctrine, by the trickery of men, in the cunning craftiness of deceitful plotting, but, speaking the truth in love, may grow up in all things into Him who is the head – Christ – from whom the whole body, joined and knit together by what every joint supplies, according to the effective working by which every part does its share, causes growth of the body for the edifying of itself in love.*

Unity strengthens our ability to have, manifest, and operate in the likeness and mind of Jesus Christ:

> ***Philippians 2:1-3*** *- If there be therefore any consolation in Christ, if any comfort of love, if any fellowship of the Spirit, if any bowels and mercies, Fulfil ye my joy, that ye be likeminded, having the same love, being of one accord, of one mind. Let nothing be done through strife or vainglory; but in lowliness of mind let each esteem other better than themselves.*

> ***Philippians 3:15-16*** *- Therefore let us, as many as are mature, have this mind; and if in anything you think otherwise, God will reveal even this to you. Nevertheless, to the degree that we have already attained, let us walk by the same rule, let us be of the same mind.*

> ***I Peter 3:8-12*** *- Finally, all of you be of one mind, having compassion for one another; love as brothers, be tenderhearted, be courteous; not returning evil for evil or reviling for reviling, but on the contrary blessing, knowing that you were called to this, that you may inherit a blessings. For He who would love life and see good days, Let*

him refrain his tongue from evil; and his lips from speaking deceit. Let him turn away from evil and do good; Let him seek peace and pursue it. For the eyes of the Lord are on the righteous, and His ears are open to their prayers; but the face of the Lord is against those who do evil.

Prayer Etiquette

- Make sure you have proper hygiene (keep mints to assist with breath, come to church smelling appropriately, avoid strong colognes and perfumes as this can be distracting and can be a trigger for those with abuse, rape, sexual or lust issues)
- Be cautious of touching. Ask people if you can touch them and if they say yes, be cautious where you touch them. Touching can cause arousal, distractions, and even trigger some past hurtful or challenging experiences. Even Jesus knew the virtue had left Him when the woman with the issue of blood touched Him so whether negative or positive, touching can spark a reaction. If it is someone of the opposite sex, try to get someone of the same sex to lay hands for you or if you feel led to lay hands, place your hand on their shoulder. It is important to be mindful of the lawsuits and sexual harassment cases and misunderstandings that are going forth in this day and age. Please use wisdom in this area.
- Don't get in a hurry.
- Wait on God to lead you in what to pray.
- Ask questions as the person will give you clues as to the reason he or she is really at the altar.
- Be sensitive to the Holy Spirit as a person may ask for prayer in one area but need prayer for something else. The Holy Spirit will reveal this to you.
- Don't feel pressured to just pray anything or to push people along when the line is built up.
- Don't be intimidated by others waiting to be prayed for. Resist temptation to rush.

- Pray until God releases you. Pray until the Spirit releases you from the prayer.
- If you see that God is still dealing with the person, encourage them to hang out at the altar until God is finished.

Seeking God During Prayer Ministry

- Never turn a person away just because they don't know what they need prayer for. Always pray for everyone that comes for ministry.
- If people don't know what they want prayer for pray in the Spirit/Pray in tongues. Seek the Holy Spirit for direction.
- Be cautious of backgrounds and traditions as some people don't understand what tongues are. So if you don't know the person or where they are coming from, be sensitive and let them know you are going to pray in your prayer language or even that you are going to pray silently so they can be in tune to what is occurring. This will help avoid confusion and offense.
- When people are unsure of what they need, wait upon God; He will give you words of wisdom and understanding.
- Don't get frustrated with prayer addicts. Prayer addicts are people who come every week for ministry. They are seeking something or may just be needed or don't know what they want, just pray for them. Let God deal with them. And even lead them in praying for their own request as this will empower them to pray rather than leaning on others.

Blessing Prayers During Times Of Uncertainty

- If you are unsure what to pray, pray a blessing prayer.
- Blessing prayers break curses.
- Blessing prayers should be done by the Holy Spirit but when done it gets the attention of the person and opens them up for more of God
- Blessing prayers are words of encouragement spoken over the person using the principles of the word or words of knowledge that the Holy Spirit gives you.
- Blessing prayers can be used when you have done all you know to do with a person but the Holy Spirit isn't done with them yet.
- If God instructs you to go pray for someone and that person is engaged in worship or praying to God, simply go up to them and begin praying, don't touch them as God could be doing something with them and you touching them will startle them and bring them out of what God is doing. Only touch them at the leading of the Holy Spirit. That way that touch will add to the ministry instead of taking away from it.
- Obey God! If He requires you to minister to a specific person, do so. If He desires for you to stay with a person until He is finished with them, do so. If He desires you to even pray for someone that is already been prayed for, do so. The work at the altar is about Him not about us.

Ministering Salvation

Here are guidelines for ministering to those in need of salvation:

Share The Need Of Salvation:
Using the Scriptures, explain that they need salvation because all have sinned.

Share God's Solution:
Using the Scriptures, share God's solution for sin, salvation by grace through faith.

Bring To A Point Of Decision:
Bring the person to a point of decision, a positive affirmation that he wants to be saved.

Pray With The Person:
Pray out loud together. Have the person confess His sins and receive Jesus Christ as Savior. If help to pray is needed, ask him to follow you in a prayer such as: *Jesus, I acknowledge that I have sinned. Please forgive me of my sin as I now repent. I take you at your Word that you forgive those who ask. I accept you as my Savior. Thank you for cleansing me from sin. In Jesus name, Amen.*

Provide Follow-Up Care:
Decision cards should be filled out on each new convert to secure their name and address for follow-up. Keep these cards somewhere in the altar area. Return completed cards to the church office for contact by the pastoral staff and referral to the discipleship class.

Questions About Salvation

Is there a difference between being sorry and repenting?
Yes. Godly sorrow worketh repentance. Being sorry or being sorry you got caught is not enough. You must repent. You must know what you did was wrong, that change is needed, and show change through your daily actions.

Why is it necessary to repent?
You must repent in order to be saved: *Repent ye therefore, and be converted, that your sins may be blotted out, when the time of refreshing shall come from the presence of the Lord. (Acts 3:19)*

Do all men need to repent?
Yes, because all have sinned. Repentance should be a daily part of our lives.

What happens if I do not repent?
I tell you...except ye repent, ye shall all likewise perish. (Luke 13:3)

Will repenting change my life?
Yes. The joy of salvation is visible along with the growth of the fruit of the Spirit: Love, joy, peace, gentleness, goodness, meekness, and faith. You will be able to live a new life.

Key Verses Regarding Salvation

o *For God so loved the world; that He gave his only begotten Son, that whosoever believeth in Him should not perish, but have everlasting life. (John 3:16)*
o *For whosoever shall call upon the name of the Lord shall be saved. (Romans 10:13)*
o *If we say that we have no sin, we deceive ourselves, and the truth is not in us. If we confess our sins, He is*

- *faithful and just to forgive us our sins, and to cleanse us from all unrighteousness. (1 John 1:8-9)*
- *But as many as received Him, to them gave he power to become the sons of God, even to them that believe on His name. (John 1:12)*
- *Behold, I stand at the door and knock; if any man hear my voice and open the door, I will come in to Him, and will sup with Him, and He with me. (Revelation 3:20)*
- *But godly sorrow worketh repentance to salvation not to be repented of; but the sorrow of the world worketh death. (2 Corinthians 7:10)*
- *I say unto you, that likewise joy shall be in heaven over one sinner that repenteth, more than over ninety and nine just persons which need no repentance. (Luke 15:7)*
- *And they went out, and preached that men should repent. (Mark 6:12)*
- *...Thus it is written, and thus it behoved Christ to suffer, and to rise from the dead the third day: And that repentance and remission of sins should be preached in His name among all nations, beginning at Jerusalem. (Luke 24:46-47)*
- *The Lord is not slack concerning His promise, as some men count slackness; but is longsuffering to us-ward, not willing that any should perish, but that all should come to repentance. (2 Peter 3:9)*
- *I tell you Nay, but except ye repent, ye shall all likewise perish. (Luke 13:3)*

Ministering To Someone Who Desires To Speak In Tongues

- Even if a person does not speak in tongues, the Holy Spirit is upon them.

    Acts 2:38 - Then Peter said unto them, Repent, and be baptized every one of you in the name of Jesus Christ for the remission of sins, and ye shall receive the gift of the Holy Ghost.

- Speaking in tongues is the voice and power of God that has come upon us, now filling in us.

    Acts 1:8 - But ye shall receive power, after that the Holy Ghost is come upon you: and ye shall be witnesses unto me both in Jerusalem, and in all Judaea, and in Samaria, and unto the uttermost part of the earth.

    Romans 15:13 - May the God of hope fill you with all joy and peace in believing, so that by the power of the Holy Spirit you may abound in hope.

    Luke 4:24 - I am going to send you what my Father has promised; but stay in the city until you have been clothed with power from on high."

- Speaking in tongues is a gift.

> *Luke 11:13 - If you then, who are evil, know how to give good gifts to your children, how much more will the heavenly Father give the Holy Spirit to those who ask him!*

- You do not have to work by tarrying for it. If you study tarrying, it is simply waiting on the Holy Spirit to empower you.
    - F. According to Scripture, the only people who ever "tarried" to receive the Holy Spirit were the one hundred and twenty who were waiting in the upper room for the coming of the Holy Spirit on the day of Pentecost. Since that day when Jesus sent the Holy Spirit in fulfillment of His promise (Acts 1:4-55), He has been present with us, available and accessible to all who open their hearts and lives to His empowering, and who are longing to receive the spiritual gifts and ministries He brings.
    - G. One of the definitions of tarry in Webster's Dictionary is to "linger with expectation." So when the 120 were in the upper room they were hanging out with the spirit of expectation. They were most likely thinking and talking on the things of God and what's to come…maybe praising and worshipping…possibly searching scriptures…but they were not tarrying in a traditional sense that we know it. They were waiting with an expectation of what Jesus said He was going to pour out, of what He said He would be leaving behind. We just want to make this clear because as we seek to minister this at the altar we do not wish

to participate in traditional religious tarrying. We want to be rooted and grounded in a scriptural foundation and divine revelation and understanding of how to be fully empowered with the Holy Spirit with the evidence of speaking in tongues.

- The bible does not say that everyone needs to speak in tongues.

    ***1Corinthians 12:30** - Have all the gifts of healing? Do all speak with tongues? Do all interpret?*

- God will not force tongues on anyone. Though He wants all to be filled with His voice and power, He will respect a person's choice in this matter.
- Speaking in tongues truly is a faith act of opening your mouth and speaking as the Holy Spirit leads.
- Through our prayer language comes an increased power and guidance of the Holy Spirit to speak the voice of God, operate in giftings and live a life of holiness.
- Without the evidence of tongues one is basically living the actions of the intimacy and comfort of the Holy Spirit without the actual intimacy and love language of having the Holy Spirit indwelling in their lives.
- One thing we will learn from our relationship with the Holy Spirit is that intimacy is power. It is motivating, refreshing, reviving, strengthening, and accelerating (just think about how you feel when you are with someone you love).
- Though one may have the Holy Spirit, without the evidence of speaking in tongues, one is limited in

their ability to express their feelings to God and God express Himself through them as the Holy Spirit makes intercession for us through groanings that we can't express or explain through our earthly comprehension or our earthly expressions.

> ***Romans 8:26*** - *Likewise the Spirit also helpeth our infirmities: for we know not what we should pray for as we ought: but the Spirit itself maketh intercession for us with groanings which cannot be uttered.*

- Also without speaking in tongues one is limited only to their native or learned language which is truly a soulish experience.
- Tongues liberate a person from the soulish to the spirit realm where they can be empowered to experience God and His mysteries on levels that the soul cannot go. This is not about the soul being carnal, but is just about when we operate in our soul, we tend to operate in our mind, will, and intellect so when we operate in this realm we tend to limit things by what we know or what feels good or what feels comfortable. However, when we operate in God from Spirit to Spirit, we are more apt to be submissive to the unknowing. All our earthly boundaries are removed and we are inside a realm of unlimited potential - where His spirit is guiding and controlling our experience in God rather than us being in control.
- Speaking in tongues elevates a believer to a place in God such that the word says God will begin to reveal mysteries to us. These mysteries cannot be revealed and sometimes even understood by those

who do not have the evidence of speaking in tongues.

> ***1Corinthians 14:2*** *- For he that speaketh in an unknown tongue speaketh not unto men, but unto God: for no man understandeth him; howbeit in the spirit he speaketh mysteries.*
>
> ***The Message Version*** *- If you praise him in the private language of tongues, God understands you but no one else does, for you are sharing intimacies just between you and him.*

Hindrances To Not Immediately Speaking In Tongues

- Fear of the manifestation of tongues itself
- Fearing the mysteries of the process of speaking in tongues
- Fear of being vulnerable (losing control) and submitting to the presence of God and giving up their need to be in control or fear of being vulnerable before others
- Fear of how they will sound or what others will say
- Fear of the intimacy of tongues because one has to surrender and be intimate with God in order to yield themselves to the experience of the Holy Spirit. The 120 was lingering…they were just waiting around for God. They deemed Him worth the wait. Many do not know how to be intimate, therefore, they fail to tap into a place of receiving.
- Tradition and religious beliefs
- Ignorance or lack of knowledge and understanding
- Not feeling worthy of God's gift
- Sin blockage or shame and guilt/condemnation still being present due to past or present sin in one's life.
- Demonic stronghold
- Fortune Telling, Satanism, Witchcraft, Horoscopes, Ouija Boards, Spiritism, or other non-Christian religions practices that need to be renounced. You see, the occult involvement in our lives was not innocent child's play. It breaks the First Commandment and gives Satan legal access to our lives. *(Deuteronomy 18:10-12)* If one is now going to seek supernatural guidance from God by His Holy Spirit, then they need to silence all other occult influences in Jesus' Name. *(Acts 19:19)* They may

even need to destroy all objects in their home or life that have supernatural ties. God speaks through our hearts not through mediums or objects.
- Atmosphere may not be conducive to being able to receive (you however can create an atmosphere by praising and worshiping or declaring the scriptures)
- Or it is not time to receive yet. Like the 120, the Holy Spirit may want to build up anticipation, faith, and/or relationship before manifesting the evidence of tongues.
- If a person is having difficulty being filled, ask the Holy Spirit to discern the reason, and keep building a relationship with Him, while asking Him to give you your prayer language. He will not leave you desiring.

> ***Luke 11:13*** *- If you then, who are evil, know how to give good gifts to your children, how much more will the heavenly Father give the Holy Spirit to those who ask him!*
>
> ***Ephesians 5:18-21*** *- And do not get drunk with wine, for that is debauchery, but be filled with the Spirit, addressing one another in psalms and hymns and spiritual songs, singing and making melody to the Lord with your heart, giving thanks always and for everything to God the Father in the name of our Lord Jesus Christ, submitting to one another out of reverence for Christ.*
>
> ***Psalms 84:11*** *- For the LORD God is a sun and shield: the LORD will give grace and glory: no good thing will he withhold from them that walk uprightly.*

2Corinthians 1:20 - *For all the promises of God in him are yea, and in him Amen, unto the glory of God by us.*

Suggestions For Leading Someone In Praying In Tongues

- There is no set in stone way to lead someone in receiving. God could give you a story to share or you may feel lead to share your own testimony of how you received the evidence of tongues. Or God may give you a revelation of how to explain it where the person can receive it. Seek the Holy Spirit and be open to moving as He desires. Have faith and He will guide you in the process.

- Below is a sketch draft we all can use to get started in leading someone in receiving:

  A. Though there is no set way standard to receive tongues, try to ensure the person is saved and water baptized first. If not lead them in these areas. And then when they get dressed from being baptized share with them about the Holy Spirit.

  B. Explain what the Holy Spirit and the evidence of speaking in tongues is.

  C. Give some scriptures to back up what you are saying and even show them in the bible if necessary. Also write scriptures down where they can study about it later if necessary.

  D. Lay hands and pray for the infilling of the Holy Spirit.

  E. Have the person ask while believing that this powerful gift is for them.

F. Have the person praise and worship and release themselves to God through their worship unto Him.

G. Worship with them while encouraging them to release themselves to God's presence. Surrendering and being open to God is key to receiving.

H. Be mindful to the atmosphere around you and what may be hindering the person from receiving if anything. If necessary stop and deal with that area.

I. Keep declaring scriptures and worship that opens up the spirit realm and release freedom and be open to lay hands and pray again as the spirit leads.

J. Run around the church yelling and screaming when they receive. I meant let myself or leadership know so we can celebrate with them.

Purpose Of Deliverance Ministry

Mark 16:15-18 - And he said unto them, Go ye into all the world, and preach the gospel to every creature. He that believeth and is baptized shall be saved; but he that believeth not shall be damned. And these signs shall follow them that believe; in my name shall they cast out devils; they shall speak with new tongues; they shall take up serpents; and if they drink any deadly thing, it shall not hurt them; they shall lay hands on the sick, and they shall recover.

Who did Jesus say were to cast out devils?

John 3:16-17 - For God so loved the world, that he gave his only begotten Son, that whosoever believeth in him should not perish, but have everlasting life. For God sent not his Son into the world to condemn the world; but that the world through him might be saved.

What does our salvation have to do with being delivered and expelling devils?

Saved in the Greek is "sozo" and means:
1. to save, deliver or protect (literally or figuratively): —
2. heal, preserve, save (self), do well, be (make) whole.
3. to save, keep safe and sound, to rescue from danger or destruction one (from injury or peril) to save a suffering one (from perishing), i. e. one suffering from disease,

4. to make well, heal, restore to health to preserve one who is in danger of destruction, to save or rescue to save in the technical
5. biblical sense negatively to deliver from the penalties of the Messianic judgment
6. to save from the evils which obstruct the reception of the Messianic deliverance

The entire reason Jesus came was to destroy the works of the devil.

Once we accept Jesus as our savior, we must receive deliverance and healing in order for the full manifestation of His works on the cross to be made manifest on our lives. It is important to embrace that deliverance is very much a part of the process for us to live a very healthy and mature life in God.

We see through the scriptures that Jesus made casting out devils a mandate for us as believers. What reasons do you think He said we should cast out demons?

We should cast out devils because:
- Jesus cast them out and said greater works than He we should do. Jesus cast them out of His people, the Israelites — the sons and daughters of Abraham — not out of the Gentiles or unbelievers.

> *Mark 1:32 - At evening, when the sun had set, they brought to Him (Jesus) all who were sick and those who were demon-possessed.*
>
> *Verses 36-38 - And Simon and those who were with Him searched for Him. When they found*

Him, they said to Him, `Everyone is looking for You.' But He said to them, `Let us go into the next towns, that I may preach there also, because for this purpose I have come forth.

***Matthew 8:16** - When evening had come they brought to Him many who were demon possessed and He cast out the spirits with a word and healed all who were sick that it might be fulfilled which was spoken by Isaiah the prophet saying, `He Himself took our infirmities and bore our sickness.*

- If we believe Jesus is our perfect pattern, then to follow Him we must do as He did, and He cast out many demons.

> ***John 14:12** -Verily, verily, I say unto you, He that believeth on me, the works that I do shall he do also; and greater works than these shall he do; because I go unto my Father.*

- If we believe then we must receive the fullness of the work of salvation. Deliverance is another manifestation of Jesus' miracle working power. People are set free when demons are expelled.
- Casting out devils is the greatest evidence of the kingdom. It is a visible supernatural manifestation of Jesus work of overcoming the enemy through the cross.

> ***Luke 11:20** - But if I cast out demons with the finger of God, surely the kingdom of God has come upon you.*

- When we cast out devils we are driving out the kingdom of the enemy and establishing the kingdom of God in its place.

Out is *"ekballō"* in the Greek and means:
1. to eject (literally or figuratively), bring forth, cast (forth, out), drive (out), expel, leave, pluck (pull, take, thrust) out, put forth (out),
2. send away (forth, out). cast out, bring forth, pull out, send forth, to send out with notion of violence
3. to drive out (cast out), to cast out (of the world), i.e. be deprived of the power and influence he exercises in the world, excrement from the belly into the sink
4. to expel a person from a society: to banish from a family
5. to compel one to depart; to bid one depart, in stern though not violent language
6. so employed that the rapid motion of the one going is transferred to the one sending forth a.to command or cause one to depart in haste
7. to draw out with force, tear out
8. with implication of force-overcoming opposite force a.to cause a thing to move straight on its intended goal
9. to reject with contempt, to cast off or away

Matt 10:5-10 - These twelve Jesus sent forth, and commanded them, saying, Go not into the way of the Gentiles, and into any city of the Samaritans enter ye not: But go rather to the lost sheep of the house of Israel. And as ye go, preach, saying, the kingdom of heaven is at hand. Heal the sick, cleanse the lepers, raise the dead, cast out devils: freely ye have received, freely give. Provide neither gold, nor silver, nor brass in your purses, nor scrip for your journey, neither two coats, neither shoes. Nor yet staves: for the workman is worthy of his meat.

Message version
Jesus sent his twelve harvest hands out with this charge: "Don't begin by traveling to some far-off place to convert unbelievers. And don't try to be dramatic by tackling some public enemy. Go to the lost, confused people right here in the neighborhood. Tell them that the kingdom is here. Bring health to the sick. Raise the dead. Touch the untouchables. Kick out the demons. You have been treated generously, so live generously. Don't think you have to put on a fund-raising campaign before you start. You don't need a lot of equipment. You are the equipment, and all you need to keep that going is three meals a day. Travel light.

- Though some demons may leave when you get born again, filled with the Holy Spirit, or during high spirit filled services, most demons don't leave willingly, so if you don't cast them out they just hang out with you, wreak havoc in your life, and depending on the demon and its assignment, eventually strive to overtake you.

In *Mark 5*, we have the man possessed with demons that lives among the tombs. The people would chain him but he would break the chains. The demons didn't leave the man because he was bound, they simply grew stronger. They cried out when Jesus came, but they did not go out until He cast them out (and with some difficulty).

> ***Mark 5:7-13*** - *But when he saw Jesus afar off, he ran and worshipped him, And cried with a loud voice, and said, What have I to do with thee, Jesus, thou Son of the most high God? I adjure thee by God, that thou torment me not. For he said unto him, Come out of the man, thou unclean spirit. And he asked him, What is thy name? And he answered, saying, My name is Legion: for we are many. And he besought him much that he would not send them away out of the country. Now there was there nigh unto the mountains a great herd of swine feeding. And all the devils besought him, saying, Send us into the swine, that we may enter into them. And forthwith Jesus gave them leave. And the unclean spirits went out, and entered into the swine: and the herd ran violently down a steep place into the sea, (they were about two thousand); and were choked in the sea.*

The challenge we have in the United States is that the demons are so embedded in our personality and culture that we have challenges discerning what a demon is, and what flesh are and soul challenges. Often the churches within America have been divided about whether a Christian can have a demon and even whether deliverance is even necessary.

However, in third world countries the supernatural and God is such a part of the culture until they freely acknowledge the existence of devils and are better able to distinguish what is a devil and what are flesh or soul challenges.

Moreover, the world at large acknowledges the manifestations of demons and admit before many Christians the existence of demons. They write songs and movies about them, conjure them up and freely share about the encounters they have with the demonic world. Yet for many of us who are to have power over such demonic forces, we tend to be afraid to embrace the possibility, and lets not even get into the possibility that it is we ourselves that just might be bound or possess a demonic spirit.

For someone who has experienced and fought demons since I was a little girl, let me tell you demons are indeed real, and if we do not assert our authority over devils, they will pridefully assert authority over us.

> **1Peter 5:8** - *Be sober, be vigilant; because your adversary the devil, as a roaring lion, walketh about, seeking whom he may devour.*
>
> **James 7:4** - *Submit yourselves, then, to God. Resist the devil, and he will flee from you.*

- Though demons can leave during praise and worship, this is not a sufficient method for thinking demons will leave:

Acts 16:16-18 - Now it happened, as we went to prayer, that a certain slave girl possessed with a spirit of divination met us, who brought her masters much profit by fortune-telling. This girl followed Paul and us, and cried out, saying, `These men are the servants of the Most High God, who proclaim to us the way of salvation.' And this she did for many days. But Paul, greatly annoyed, turned and said to the spirit, `I command you in the name of Jesus Christ to come out of her.' And he came out that very hour.

Luke 13:11-13 - And, behold, there was a woman which had a spirit of infirmity eighteen years, and was bowed together, and could in no wise lift up herself. And when Jesus saw her, he called her to him, and said unto her, Woman, thou art loosed from thine infirmity. And he laid his hands on her: and immediately she was made straight, and glorified God.

In both these instances, the people were in the presence of God. Yet they still were bound. They had to receive direct ministry to be delivered from demonic bondage.

- We cast out demons because we have been given victory over them. Jesus desires us to operate in zeal, compassion, and the power and authority of the Lord. This is what compels us to walk in His shoes by casting out devils.

    Luke 9:1 – Then he called His twelve disciples together and gave them power and authority over all demons, and to cure diseases.

Luke 10:19 - *Behold, I give you the authority to trample on serpents and scorpions, and over all the power of the enemy, and nothing shall by any means hurt you.*

Acts 10:38 - *How God anointed Jesus of Nazareth with the Holy Spirit and with power, and He went about doing good and healing all who were oppressed with the devil, because God was with Him.*

He was given that power and authority and now He lives in us. What He is, He is in us.

1John 3:8 - *He that committeth sin is of the devil; for the devil sinneth from the beginning. For this purpose the Son of God was manifested, that he might destroy the works of the devil.*

Demonic Manifestations

How do you know if you or someone else has a demon?

Some ways to detect demon manifestation: (From Streams of truth website)
First: Lack of control in any part or life — of what you think or do. If your emotions are out of control or you are addictive, you may have a demon. The flesh has taken on a passenger that is now exercising you to want or do beyond your ability to stop.

Second: Moods, mood swings, emotional roller coasters, and/or depression are evidence of demons. Although medicine wants to attribute such to chemical imbalances, we have clearly seen that it is simply a choice of the will. We choose to receive a spirit into our life that provides the mood. (For more about this, we have a tape about deliverance from depression.)

Third: Living in the past or the future. The church has been doing this. We hear and read so much about "when." We live now, not "when." There is no promise of tomorrow. If everything is for tomorrow, we may miss it. We have already missed what is past. What about today? Is there any victory today? Is there anything to praise God for now? Can we know and see God's Hand today, or must we wait until the rapture or something else? Living in the past or future is demonic. It is the subtle work of demons in your life and in your mind.

Fourth: Difficulty exercising yourself as a believer — Having trouble praying, studying the Bible, praising or walking in the principles of God. Often stumbling and have difficulty doing the things that God calls you to do is evidence of the demonic working to hinder you. Every believer should be able and want to pray, study God's Word, freely raise their hands and be clamorously foolish before God. One should be able to dance, sing and rejoice in the Lord without any limitations or self-consciousness. If you cannot, you may need deliverance. If God wants me to be *hallalling* (which means to be clamorously foolish before Him) Him, then I should be free to do it. If I need to get on my knees or fall on my face or whatever I need to do in the presence of anybody I should be free enough in Christ to do it. If not, I need help.

Fifth: Continual defeat in external areas — in finances, in family relations, in health, in possessions — indicates there's a "booger" working. Where is this thing? It's in you. Anytime we are conscious of what we're doing or how we're talking or what we are saying, and we are aware that something is not right, we're discerning a demonic thing in our life — If I'm talking too much, what is prompting me to do this? What is exercising me to do this? We are called to liberty and victory not such bondage! Wake up, Saint, it's time to possess the land!

1John 4:1-3 - Beloved, do not believe every spirit, but test the spirits to see whether they are from God, for many false prophets have gone out into the world. By this you know the Spirit of God: every spirit that confesses that Jesus Christ has come in the flesh is from God, and every spirit that does not confess Jesus is not from God. This is the spirit of the antichrist, which you heard was coming and now is in the world already.

John 10:10 - The thief comes only to steal and kill and destroy. I came that they may have life and have it abundantly.

Ephesians 6:10-18 - Finally, be strong in the Lord and in the strength of his might. Put on the whole armor of God, that you may be able to stand against the schemes of the devil. For we do not wrestle against flesh and blood, but against the rulers, against the authorities, against the cosmic powers over this present darkness, against the spiritual forces of evil in the heavenly places. Therefore take up the whole armor of God, that you may be able to withstand in the evil day, and having done all, to stand firm. Stand therefore, having fastened on the belt of truth, and having put on the breastplate of righteousness.

1Peter 5:8 - Be sober, be vigilant; because your adversary the devil, as a roaring lion, walks about, seeking whom he may devour:

How to Cast Out Demons

The importance of "In the name of Jesus:"

How did Jesus' disciples go about casting out demons? Through His name. **Luke 10:17** tells us, *"And the seventy returned again with joy, saying, Lord, even the devils are subject unto us through thy name."*

How did the early church go about casting out demons? Through His name. **Acts 16:18** tells us a story where Paul, *"turned and said to the spirit, I command thee in the name of Jesus Christ to come out of her. And he came out the same hour."*

How are the believers today supposed to be casting out demons? Through His name. As we can see in **Mark 16:17**, *"these signs shall follow them that believe; in my name shall they cast out devils."*

Authority is exercised through faith:

Matthew 17:19-20, *"Then came the disciples to Jesus apart, and said, why could not we cast him out? And Jesus said unto them, Because of your unbelief..."* Obviously they had the authority, but they weren't able to use it because their level of faith wasn't high enough to access the level of authority that needed to be exercised to drive out that particular kind of unclean spirit. Some evil spirits are stronger and harder to drive out, and sometimes prayer and fasting is necessary to build our faith up so we can drive them out, as we can see in the next *verse 21, "Howbeit this kind goeth not out but by prayer and fasting."*

Other Methods of Deliverance

1. We can use our prayer language as we pray for the person. Demons fear the use of this language.
2. We can quote from the Word of God and use the authority of the Word of God to command the spirit to leave
3. Anointing with oil is very effective as we pray.
4. Ask the person to praise and worship God. As they praise and worship, any demonic power within them will begin to leave.
5. We should ask the Holy Spirit to anoint us before and as we are praying.
6. The power of love will break the strongholds of demons. Sometimes you may need to hug a person or just speak over them their love and worth in God.
7. The power of blessings over a person will break curses, generational holds and cause demons to loose. Be open to spending time speaking blessings over the person and declaring what God is saying about the person.
8. Listen to what the Holy Spirit is telling us as to how we should pray.
9. Ensure the person understands that God loves them and accepts them.
    Ephesians 1:6 - *To the praise of the glory of His grace, by which He has made us accepted in the Beloved.*
10. Sometimes we need to fast for demons to leave us or to prepare to deliver others.
11. There should be a renouncing of all sin and unbelief on the part of the person being counseled.

12. Encourage the person to call on the name of Jesus
    Romans 10:13 - *For whoever calls on the name of the LORD shall be saved.*
13. We should agree with other persons to bind the spirit and loose the person from it.
    Matthew 18:18-19 - *Assuredly, I say to you, whatever you bind on earth will be bound in heaven, and whatever you loose on earth will be loosed in heaven. Again I say to you that if two of you agree on earth concerning anything that they ask, it will be done for them by My Father in heaven.*
14. We should plead the blood of Jesus Christ, i.e. remind the devil that through the blood of Jesus Christ we have been cleansed, redeemed, sanctified and justified.
15. The person being ministered to should assert their will and resist the devil.

<u>References:</u>
The Holy Bible in different versions
Dictionary.com
Merriam Webster's Online Dictionary
Strong's Concordance

Reasons Demons Stay

- They are usually simply an indication that there are deeper issues or root causes. You can remove the demon, but if you do not remove the root something else just comes in. Maybe a generational curse needs to be broken, inner healing is needed, or the person is in agreement with the demon and needs to renounce or break ties with it.
- God will allow demons to stay to reveal the real problem or generational stronghold. God may want to take the person through a process of healing.
- God may want to teach the person how to operate in deliverance or grow them in their giftings, calling, or authority so He is using His relationship with them to teach them.
- The presence of demons serves as a signpost that gives direction to what needs to be healed.
- Authority over demons is not screaming or loudness-it is not voice tone. (All yelling does is let demons know you are insecure). Demons do not respond to loudness but authority. Know and walk in your authority and do not allow a stubborn demon to make you angry where you SHIFT into operating in agitation and insecurity.
- Be legalistic with demonic spirits (If demons are loud tell them to be quiet and if they refuse tell them they are defying Christ) (Tell them they have defied the Lord Jesus Christ and to Go!)
- Sometimes it can be the person themselves who is going ballistic during deliverance ministry, and not the demons. You may be struggling with that person, simply take them to a side room and ALWAYS TAKE ANOTHER PERSON WITH YOU WHEN YOU GO; NEVER GO BY YOURSELF! Pray

peace over them and explain what is happening to them and that they have nothing to be afraid of as God is a comforter and deliverance is available to set them free. Talk them through each step of the deliverance process and be sensitive in knowing that they may not be ready to be delivered.

References:
The Holy Bible in different versions
Dictionary.com
Merriam Webster's Online Dictionary
Strong's Concordance

Kingdom Shifters Books & Apparel
Available at Kingdomshifters.com

BOOKS FOR EVERYONE

Healing The Wounded Leader

Kingdom Shifters Decree That Thang

There Is An App For That

Kingdom Watchman Builder On the Wall

Embodiment Of A Kingdom Watchman Releasing The Vision

Dismantling Homosexuality Handbook Feasting In His Presence

Kingdom Heirs Decree That Thing

Let There Be Sight

Atmosphere Changers (Weaponry

BOOKS FOR DANCERS

Dancers! Dancers! Decree That Thang

Spirits That Attack Dance Ministers & Ministries

TEE SHIRTS

Kingdom Shifters Tee Shirt

Let The Fruit Speak Tee Shirt

Releasing The Vision Tee Shirt

Kingdom Perspective Tee Shirt

Stand in Position Tee Shirt

No Defense Tee Shirt

My God Rules Like A Boss Tee Shirt

Destiny Blueprint Tee Shirt

CD'S

Decree That Thing CD

Kingdom Heirs Decree That Thing CD

Teachings & Worship CD's

www.ingramcontent.com/pod-product-compliance
Lightning Source LLC
Chambersburg PA
CBHW061248040426
42444CB00010B/2292